S. Hrg. 115–187

THE GLOBAL NUCLEAR WEAPONS ENVIRONMENT

HEARING

BEFORE THE

COMMITTEE ON ARMED SERVICES
UNITED STATES SENATE

ONE HUNDRED FIFTEENTH CONGRESS

FIRST SESSION

MARCH 8, 2017

Printed for the use of the Committee on Armed Services

Available via the World Wide Web: http://www.fdsys.gov/

U.S. GOVERNMENT PUBLISHING OFFICE

28–965 PDF   WASHINGTON : 2018

For sale by the Superintendent of Documents, U.S. Government Publishing Office
Internet: bookstore.gpo.gov Phone: toll free (866) 512–1800; DC area (202) 512–1800
Fax: (202) 512–2104 Mail: Stop IDCC, Washington, DC 20402–0001

(II)

CONTENTS

MARCH 8, 2017

(III)

THE GLOBAL NUCLEAR WEAPONS ENVIRONMENT

WEDNESDAY, MARCH 8, 2017

U.S. SENATE,
SUBCOMMITTEE ON STRATEGIC FORCES,
COMMITTEE ON ARMED SERVICES,
Washington, DC.

The subcommittee met, pursuant to notice, at 2:32 p.m. in Room SR–222, Russell Senate Office Building, Senator Deb Fischer (chair of the subcommittee) presiding.

Committee members present: Senators Fischer, Inhofe, Cotton, Donnelly, Heinrich, Warren, and Peters.

OPENING STATEMENT OF SENATOR DEB FISCHER

Senator FISCHER. Welcome. The hearing will come to order.

We have just had a vote called here in the Senate, so we are going to have a 15-minute recess so members of the committee can vote, and then we will come back and start the hearing.

So, we are in recess. Thank you.

[Recess.]

Senator FISCHER. The committee will come to order.

The committee meets today to receive testimony on the global nuclear weapons environment. As the first formal hearing of the Strategic Forces Subcommittee for this year, the objective is to set the stage for the committee's review of the President's fiscal year 2018 budget request as it pertains to nuclear matters.

We are joined today by three well-known former Government officials, all experts in the field of nuclear deterrence and arms control.

Dr. Keith Payne was the principal architect of the 2001 Nuclear Posture Review in the George W. Bush Defense Department.

Dr. Gary Samore served as Senior Advisor to President Obama on nuclear and arms control policy.

Retired Air Force General Robert Kehler is our military expert, having served as Commander of U.S. Strategic Command.

This hearing comes as the Administration begins work on a new Nuclear Posture Review. I believe the policy foundations of our nuclear deterrent and modernization programs remain sound, and I agree with the hope you expressed in your opening statement, General Kehler, that, quote, "The upcoming Nuclear Posture Review validates these plans and restates the urgency needed to carry them out."

(1)

I look forward to hearing more from our witnesses about their perspectives on the NPR and what they believe the key objectives or considerations should be.

I'd also like to welcome the new members we have on this committee. I look forward to working with each of you and continuing the bipartisan consensus on the need for modernizing our nuclear enterprise.

With that, I would like to turn to our ranking member, Senator Donnelly, for any opening remarks he would care to make.

STATEMENT OF SENATOR JOE DONNELLY

Senator DONNELLY. Thank you, Madam Chair. I want to start today by welcoming you as the new Chair of our subcommittee. Senator Fischer has been a leader on many of these issues for years, and I look forward to working together with you to maintain our strong bipartisan consensus on the importance of the U.S. nuclear deterrent and the need for continued U.S. leadership on nuclear non-proliferation.

Let me also thank our witnesses for joining us today to talk about the state of some of the world's nuclear powers, not just Russia and China but North Korea, India, and Pakistan. We've asked our witnesses to review and assess what has changed in the world since the last Nuclear Posture Review in 2010.

We know Russia has become increasingly aggressive toward the United States and our allies. We now have public reports of serious violations of the [Intermediate Range Nuclear Forces] INF Treaty, a landmark agreement signed by President Reagan and Mikhail Gorbachev in 1987.

Likewise, we have reports that North Korea is within reach of developing an [intercontinental ballistic missile] ICBM. Whether that missile can carry a nuclear warhead is still in debate, but we must prepare for the worst case.

Meanwhile, China is developing a nuclear-armed submarine to patrol the Pacific, holding the United States at risk and impacting the stability of South and Southeast Asia.

These are all troubling developments that have come to the fore since the 2010 [Nuclear Posture Review] NPR. I look forward to the testimony of our witnesses on these pressing issues and their implications for U.S. national security.

Before I close, I want to note that over the past several Congresses we have worked hard to keep the modernization of our nuclear deterrent bipartisan. This involves recapitalizing all three legs of our triad over the next 20 years and major life extension programs for our warheads. Our planned nuclear modernization is a long-term acquisition program, and we cannot lose sight of the fundamental importance of this ongoing effort as we move forward in this Congress.

The young airmen in the ICBM fields and on our bombers, and sailors on deterrence patrol at sea, are counting on us to replace their aging systems. I hope we can meet their expectations and get them the modernized triad they so badly need.

I want to thank all of our new members. Welcome aboard.

Thank you, and I look forward to today's briefing.

Senator FISCHER. Thank you, Senator Donnelly.

We now turn to our witnesses. Your full statements will be made part of the record, so I ask that you provide brief opening comments of four to five minutes, after which we will proceed with seven-minute rounds.

General Kehler, welcome. Nice to see you.

STATEMENT OF GENERAL C. ROBERT KEHLER, USAF [RET.], FORMER COMMANDER, UNITED STATES STRATEGIC COMMAND

General KEHLER. Thank you, Madam Chair. Nice to see you as well, and thank you for inviting me. Senator Donnelly, thanks to you as well, sir, and thanks to the members of the subcommittee. I say this in my prepared remarks, but this subcommittee provided an awful lot of support to me personally when I served at Strategic Command and before that at Air Force Space Command, and especially to the men and women that I was privileged to command. Thank you for all of that.

I am going to be presenting my personal perspective today, having taken the uniform off now a couple of years ago. I'm not representing the Department or STRATCOM or the Air Force today. I'm representing my own views and opinions. To preserve as much time as possible for your questions, I just want to highlight three points for you to consider.

First, as tempting as it is to call today's situation a new Cold War, I think it's very important to remember that we live in far more complicated and uncertain times today. The diverse strategic threat that we face is far more complex than the singular threat we faced during the Cold War. To effectively deter dangerous actors who have widely different motives, objectives, and capabilities requires us to carefully tailor our deterrent strategies, our plans, and our capabilities to match them. One size does not fit all. To effectively assure our allies and partners of the extended deterrence guarantee requires us to coordinate our strategies and plans with their unique perspectives and needs as well.

Second, nuclear weapons are not gone from world affairs, and it doesn't look to me like they're going to be gone anytime soon. Since the end of the Cold War, the United States has deemphasized the role and prominence of our nuclear weapons. Along with Russia, we have dramatically reduced the number of deployed weapons and supporting stockpile. We've postured the remaining force to be far less aggressive than what I experienced when I began serving in the mid-1970s.

Combat experience has shown us that conventional and other forces can now be realistically considered in some scenarios and again some potential targets where nuclear weapons were once the preferred or, in some cases, the only approach. We don't have to rely on our nuclear weapons in quite the same way today as we did during the Cold War, without question. Twenty-first Century strategic deterrence must be based on more than nuclear capabilities.

Nevertheless, nuclear weapons continue to perform a critical foundational role in our defense strategy and the strategies of our allies and partners. Nuclear weapons remain the ultimate guarantor of our national survival. Nuclear weapons prevent the coercive and, more importantly, the actual use of nuclear weapons against us and our allies. Nuclear weapons constrain the scope and scale of conflict. Nuclear weapons obviate the need for our allies to acquire their own. Nuclear weapons force potential adversary leaders to stop and ponder the consequences of their actions before they act. In my personal view, history shows that no other weapons have the same deterrent effect as nuclear weapons.

Third, the U.S. is at a critical point regarding the future of our nuclear capability. Over the last 10 years we have conducted 18 to 20 studies—it depends on which ones you count—on our nuclear posture and our nuclear forces and the issues that we've had in our nuclear forces. Some of those I participated in directly, by the way, and all have said the same thing: the systems are at the end of their service lives. We are rapidly expending whatever margins are left, and we are out of time.

Over the last few years a basic consensus has emerged between the executive and the legislative branches regarding the way ahead to modernize the weapons, the delivery platforms, the critical infrastructure that supports them, and the supporting command, control, and communications systems. In my view, the most important step Congress can take is to get on with it.

Finally, clarity and consistency are as important now as they ever were during the Cold War. In my personal observation, since the end of the Cold War policymakers across administrations have sent conflicting signals regarding the continued value of the U.S. nuclear deterrent and the necessity and cost of its modernization. Committing to the plan and moving forward to execute it will do much to demonstrate our resolve. Deterrence credibility demands it.

Again, Madam Chair, thank you for inviting me, and I look forward to your questions.

[The prepared statement of General Kehler follows:]

PREPARED STATEMENT BY GENERAL C. ROBERT KEHLER

Chairman Fischer, Ranking Member Donnelly, and distinguished members of the subcommittee, I am honored to join you today to offer my personal perspective on the global nuclear weapons environment. The views I express today are mine and do not represent the Department of Defense, United States Strategic Command, or the United States Air Force.

As I begin I want to thank you for the support you provided to me and the people I was privileged to command while I served at Air Force Space Command and United States Strategic Command, and for your continued focus on these important matters.

21ST CENTURY SECURITY ENVIRONMENT

We live in highly uncertain and complex times and I continue to believe that a robust strategic deterrent composed of missile defenses, leading-edge conventional and non-kinetic capabilities, modern nuclear forces, assured command and control, effective intelligence collection and support, and highly trained and well-led people will be needed to underwrite U.S. national security and to assure the security of our allies and partners for as far into the future as I can see.

Threats to our security and the security of our allies are diverse, can arrive at our doorsteps quickly, and can range from small arms in the hands of terrorists to nuclear weapons in the hands of hostile state leaders. Yesterday's regional battlefield is becoming tomorrow's global battle-space where conflicts may begin in cyberspace and quickly extend to space ... most likely before traditional air, land, and sea forces are engaged. Adversaries are acquiring technologies and exploiting the interconnected nature of our world to quickly transit political, geographic, and physical boundaries. The possible intersection of violent extremism and weapons of mass destruction remains a significant concern that requires constant vigilance.

State and non-state actors alike stress our intelligence capabilities and contingency plans by employing highly adaptive, hybrid combinations of strategies, tactics, and capabilities and by using the speed of information to further their cause and mask their activities behind a veil of deception and ambiguity. New capabilities like cyber weapons and unmanned vehicles are emerging and familiar weapons like ballistic missiles and advanced conventional capabilities are more available, affordable, and lethal.

Current events remind us that we must continue to pursue and destroy violent extremists and their networks while remaining constantly on guard to prevent and respond to attacks from them. Beyond violent extremists, state adversaries are seeking to change the strategic situation in their favor by threatening the U.S. and allied homelands below the nuclear threshold with attack by long-range conventional and cyber weapons, while preserving the capability to escalate to nuclear weapons with a variety of options from limited to major attacks.

This type of "integrated" strategic threat is completely different from the Cold War when strategic attack was synonymous with nuclear attack. When used in concert with capabilities designed to degrade our key operational enablers (e.g., space-based ISR and communications) and negate our conventional power projection capabilities, state adversaries believe a credible threat to escalate a conflict to the strategic level against the U.S. Homeland and the homelands of our allies will raise the risks and costs of U.S. intervention to unacceptable levels, force the U.S. to the sidelines, fracture our alliances, and thereby enable more assertive foreign policies and aggressive actions. Nuclear weapons underwrite their approach.

Even discounting for hyperbole, recent public reports validate what I saw while on active duty. Violent extremists continue to evolve and present an active threat. Russia and China are both upgrading their significant long-range conventional strike capabilities and exercise them routinely; both are active in cyberspace; both are deploying the means to threaten our national security space assets; both are improving their anti-access/area denial capabilities to challenge our forward-deployed and power projection forces; and both can quickly inflict enormous casualties and damage on the U.S. and our allies with nuclear forces that they are modernizing. Although I believe the likelihood of a massive surprise nuclear attack is low today (and still must be deterred), I am troubled by statements from Russia and elsewhere that describe the possible limited use of nuclear weapons in regional conflicts.

Beyond Russia and China, North Korea routinely threatens its regional neighbors, United States territory, and United States forward forces with conventional and nuclear attack and is aggressively working to deploy its weapons on intercontinental-class missiles to threaten the United States directly. India and Pakistan raise the potential of nuclear use in their disputes. Active conflict and unrest continue elsewhere.

In my view, we cannot deal with any of today's adversaries in a "one size fits all" manner. Deterring dangerous actors with widely different motivations, objectives, and capabilities requires us to carefully tailor our strategies, plans and capabilities. Deterrence strategies that are the preferred ways to counter a nation-state will likely not be effective against violent extremists where direct action is often the only recourse. Nuclear weapons may not be the most credible deterrence tool in some scenarios where they were once the preferred (sometimes the only) option. Therefore, we must match our strategies, plans, and capabilities to individual actors and deploy a range of conventional, non-kinetic, and nuclear capabilities that can either deter (always the preferred outcome) or, if necessary, defeat them in multiple scenarios. Similarly, we must also synchronize our extended deterrence strategies and plans with the unique needs of our allies and partners.

THE ENDURING ROLE OF U.S. NUCLEAR WEAPONS

A long-held view of deterrence theory suggests that deterrence exists when an adversary believes they cannot achieve their objectives, will suffer unacceptable consequences if they try, or both. It is based on an adversary's understanding of the capability and resolve of their potential enemy. Ultimately, deterrence is about human beings, what they value, and what they believe.

The end of the Cold War allowed the U.S. to reduce the role and prominence of nuclear weapons in our defense planning and to dramatically reduce both the number of deployed weapons and the overall size of our stockpile. As several of my predecessors at United States Strategic Command and I recently stated: "Today's nuclear triad is far smaller and postured much less aggressively than its Cold War ancestor. Shaped by presidential initiatives and arms reduction agreements, by 2018 the number of weapons deployed on triad systems will be barely one-tenth of Cold War highs. Heavy bombers and supporting tankers are no longer loaded and poised to take off with nuclear weapons, and ballistic missiles are aimed at open areas of the ocean. Theater nuclear forces have been reduced to a small number of dual-capable aircraft supporting the NATO alliance." [1] In addition, policymakers have refined the U.S. position on the potential use of nuclear weapons (extreme circumstances where vital national interests are at stake) and have restated the U.S. commitment to the negative security guarantee contained in the Nuclear Non-Proliferation Treaty.

Nevertheless, nuclear weapons continue to play a critical role in our security strategy and the strategies of our key allies and partners as the ultimate guarantor of national survival. While no longer needed to deter a conventional attack from the massed armored formations of the now extinct Warsaw Pact, nuclear weapons continue to prevent both the coercive and actual use of these weapons against us (their primary objective), constrain the scope and scale of conflict, obviate the need for additional allies and partners to acquire their own, and compel potential adversary leaders to consider the implications of their actions before they act. Highly precise conventional weapons, non-kinetic capabilities, and defenses all play an increased deterrent role today; but I believe history shows that conventional weapons have never had the same overall deterrent effect as nuclear weapons and, therefore, cannot serve as a large-scale replacement. The ultimate paradox of the nuclear age is still with us—to prevent their use, we must remain credibly prepared to use them.

GOING FORWARD

The Cold War has been over for more than 25 years and as tempting as it is to look backward to that time as the basis for today's solutions (especially those involving nuclear weapons), we must recognize that little in today's world is the same. I am concerned when I hear the words *new cold war* used to describe either the current situation or a suggestion of our response to it. While many of the concepts sound the same, how we understand our adversaries and develop approaches to deter them must be based on a clear-eyed assessment of them and the realities of the 21st Century; not the mid-point of the 20th Century. Nuclear weapons remain foundational to our security, but nuclear weapons are only one of many important instruments that must be carefully orchestrated for maximum deterrent credibility and effect today.

U.S. nuclear strategy and policy have been remarkably consistent over the decades. Changes have been evolutionary and not revolutionary and, thus, I believe the United States and Russia have been able to establish a pathway that has dramatically reduced the nuclear threat while maintaining stability and deterrence credibility. Arms reduction and other efforts have verifiably reduced the stockpiles while promoting mutual visibility and understanding. Nuclear policy and employment strategy have been revised to meet today's deterrence needs, including the full consideration of conventional and non-kinetic strike capabilities in plans and options. Nuclear weapons are not gone from world affairs and are not likely to be gone anytime soon. The U.S. is at a critical juncture regarding the future of our nuclear deterrent and, as numerous studies and reports have shown, we are out of margin.

The time to act has arrived. Again, as my colleagues and I recently said: "The last concentrated investment to modernize the triad came during the Reagan administration. We continue to rely on that era's Ohio-class ballistic missile submarines (SSBNs), missiles, and B–2 bombers today as well as B–52s, Minuteman ICBMs, Air Launched Cruise Missiles (ALCMs), and command and control systems that were designed and fielded far earlier. Even with periodic upgrades and life extensions, legacy systems that were conceived and deployed over three decades ago are reaching the inevitable end of their service lives." [2]

A bipartisan consensus to modernize the triad, dual-capable aircraft, the nuclear weapons industrial complex, and the nuclear command/control/communications system has been carefully built between the Department of Defense and Congress. I fully support the triad and the nuclear modernization proposals that have been described in recent budgets, and hope the upcoming Nuclear Posture Review validates these plans and restates the sense of urgency needed to carry them out.

The modernization plans that are before you address the significant issues that exist in the nuclear enterprise. Weapon life extension programs will ensure the de-

---

[1] Gen. C. Robert Kehler, Gen. Larry D. Welch, Adm. James O. Ellis, Gen. Kevin P. Chilton, Adm. Cecil D. Haney, Adm. Henry G. Chiles, Gen. Eugene E. Habiger, Adm. Richard W. Mies, Open Letter, "The U. S. Nuclear Triad Needs an Upgrade," *The Wall Street Journal*, 12 January 2017, p. A17.

[2] Ibid.

ployed force remains safe, secure, and effective. Modernizing the unique and highly specialized nuclear weapon industrial complex will sustain the deployed force and, with adoption of the 3+2 strategy, will allow us to further reduce the stockpile while retaining the critical capabilities and skills needed to respond to an uncertain future. Revitalizing the triad and dual-capable aircraft will continue to present an attacker with insurmountable attack and defensive problems along with the certainty of an effective response, provide the president with a range of options to deal with a crisis or conflict, and provide an effective hedge against technical failures or geopolitical uncertainty. Upgrading the nuclear command, control, and communications system will ensure the president remains linked to the forces for positive control.

In addition to the modernization plans already proposed, I would also highlight several other important needs for your consideration.

- Better adaptive planning capabilities to meet emerging (and possibly unforeseen) scenarios in a crisis or conflict.
- Increased attention to new threats like cyber weapons, inside actors, and drones.
- More emphasis on enhancing the resilience of critical space and network infrastructures.
- More effective integration of cross-domain capabilities.
- Prototyping and other steps to retain critical skills in nuclear weapon design and manufacture.

While I think the renewed discussion about strategic deterrence and nuclear weapons is long overdue, such discussion can become harmful if the result is confusion or paralysis. In my estimation, policy makers across several administrations have sent conflicting signals regarding the continued value of the U.S. nuclear deterrent and the necessity and cost of its modernization. Clarity and commitment regarding nuclear weapons, their continued foundational role in U.S. and allied defense strategy, and the investment needed to sustain them are as important now as they ever were during the Cold War. Deterrence credibility and national security demand it.

Senator FISCHER. Thank you, General.
Dr. Payne, welcome.

STATEMENT OF DR. KEITH B. PAYNE, PROFESSOR AND DEPARTMENT HEAD, DEFENSE STRATEGIC STUDIES, MISSOURI STATE UNIVERSITY

Dr. PAYNE. Thank you, Madam Chair. It's an honor to speak here today, and I too am presenting my own personal views.

The starting point for my remarks is to observe that the threat environment has worsened dramatically since the 2010 Nuclear Posture Review. Moscow is now highly motivated to correct the perceived geopolitical injustices supposedly forced on it by the West during the Cold War. The Putin regime is rearming Russia and changing European borders, with the goals of overturning the despised Western post-Cold War order and restoring Russia's power position.

Further, Russia believes it has exploitable political and military advantages that enable it to coerce and deter the West with nuclear first-strike threats or limited nuclear employment. These perceived advantages, combined with Moscow's doubts about [North Atlantic Treaty Organization] NATO's resolve, now threaten deterrence and our key allies.

This is not speculation about some dark future; it is here, and it is now. President Putin has boasted recently that he could have Russian troops in five NATO capitals in two days. What are the implications of these beliefs for Western deterrence requirements?

First, the West must end Russian misperceptions that limited nuclear employment is a winning strategy, and that Moscow's resolve and readiness to break the West are greater than the West's resolve and readiness to prevent it from doing so. We can help in this regard with declaratory policies and relevant exercises that signal Western resolve and capabilities in Moscow.

In addition, a basic need is for U.S. nuclear and conventional forces of sufficient size and flexibility to adapt, as necessary and over time, to an increasingly hostile and very surprising threat environment. Western efforts to deploy high-readiness non-nuclear defense capabilities for NATO frontline states will likely reduce Moscow's perceptions of exploitable advantage and strengthen the credibility of our extended deterrence commitments.

Eight additional steps I'll mention in this regard include, first, modernizing the U.S. nuclear triad, possibly to include some very low-yield missile options, and strengthening U.S. command and control systems.

Second, deploy national ballistic missile defense to defeat any possible limited nuclear attack strategy. This is important given North Korean mounting capabilities in this regard.

Third, advancing the delivery date of the nuclear capable F–35 and B61–12.

Fourth, retaining the unique capabilities of the B61–11.

Fifth, increasing NATO DCA, dual-capable aircraft, survivability and readiness.

Sixth, expanding DCA burden-sharing among NATO allies.

Seventh, increasing the active and passive defense of key NATO nodes and assets.

Eighth, ensuring that NATO conventional forces can fight and survive in the context of limited Russian nuclear strikes.

Finally, the development of new U.S. nuclear capabilities should not be ruled out or crimped early by policy.

Increased U.S. nuclear force numbers may well be unnecessary, but the currently planned nuclear force posture was deemed adequate in 2010 on the assumptions that, one, Russia would abide by its arms control agreements; and two, that there would be no call for additional capabilities. The Russians have now violated that former condition, and the latter is now open to question.

There's much more to say about these issues, but to stay within time I'll stop here and look forward to your questions.

[The prepared statement of Dr. Payne follows:]

PREPARED STATEMENT BY DR. KEITH B. PAYNE

The forthcoming Nuclear Posture Review (NPR) will confront two overarching questions: First: what are the changes in the security environment since the 2010 NPR? Second, what do these changes suggest regarding U.S. policies and requirements?

My remarks along these lines today focus on Russia, but there are important parallels with regard to United States–Chinese relations that we can discuss as well.

The most fundamental point is that threat conditions have worsened dramatically since the 2010 NPR. Indeed, each of the three previous NPRs presumed an increasingly benign new world order in which nuclear weapons and deterrence would play a declining role. The predominant view was that the post-Cold War world was moving beyond nuclear weapons, and that nuclear deterrence was increasingly irrelevant to United States relations with Russia and China.[1] In this more benign new

---

[1] It is difficult to overstate the certainty that attended this policy direction. It was reflected in a highly-regarded 1991 *Foreign Affairs* article written by three senior former officials and authors, including the late Robert McNamara. To wit, hostility with Russia was described as,

world the highest priority of U.S. nuclear policy was nonproliferation and the reduction of U.S. nuclear forces and their roles was deemed critical to advance that priority goal.[2]

The overarching U.S. policy direction that followed from these beliefs was that U.S. nuclear forces and deterrence were of greatly-declining value, and correspondingly, their salience and numbers should be lowered on a continuing and progressive basis.

Unfortunately, it is now clear that the expected benign new world order has been overtaken by reality,[3] including particularly blatant Russian and Chinese drives to overturn the existing political order in Europe and Asia respectively, and the decade-long expansion of nuclear capabilities pursued by both Moscow and Beijing. Today's stark reality is demonstrated by Russia's call for a new "post-West" world order,[4] its continuing aggression against Ukraine and explicit nuclear first-use threats against NATO states and neutrals.[5]

The Putin regime has sought repeatedly to coerce the West with threats of nuclear first-use employment. According to Russian military writings and exercises, as reported, the West is expected to concede in the face of Russian nuclear escalation threats or limited nuclear first use.[6]

Correspondingly, Russia is not interested in limiting its theater conventional or nuclear forces and has deployed a nuclear-capable cruise missile, reportedly the SSC–8, in direct violation of the 1987 INF Treaty.[7] According to Col. Gen. Sergei Ivanov, then-Kremlin Chief of Staff, Russia has little incentive for further nuclear arms control negotiations with the United States because Russian systems "are relatively new" while the United States has "not conducted any upgrades for a long time."[8] Unfortunately, this type of characterization of U.S. nuclear arms is not controversial.[9]

"hardly more likely to be revived than the religious wars of the sixteenth and seventeenth centuries between Catholics and Protestants in Europe," Carl Kaysen, Robert S. McNamara, and George W. Rathjens, "Nuclear Weapons After the Cold War," *Foreign Affairs,* Vol. 70, No. 4 (Fall 1991), p. 96. Over two decades later, the Global Zero Commission study, chaired by a former Vice Chairman of the JCS, similarly said, "The risk of nuclear confrontation between the United States and either Russia or China belongs to the past, not the future." James Cartwright, Chair, Global Zero U.S. Nuclear Policy Commission, *Modernizing U.S. Nuclear Strategy,Force Structure and Posture* (Washington, D.C.: Global Zero, May 2012), p. 6, available at http://www.globalzero.org/files/gz_us_nuclear_policy_commission_report.pdf.

[2] U.S. Department of Defense, 2010 Nuclear Posture Review Report (Washington, D.C.: Department of Defense, April 2010), pp. i, iii-vii, available at https://www.defense.gov/Portals/1/features/defenseReviews/NPR/2010_Nuclear_Posture_Review_Report.pdf.

[3] So much so that Sweden has decided to return to military conscription, and the Swedish Defense Minister, Peter Hultquist, has acknowledged: "Politicians at the time maybe thought that the future would be more sunny than the reality is today … The security situation and what could come in the future was underestimated." See Martin Selsoe Sorensen, "Sweden Reinstates Conscription, With an Eye on Russia," *The New York Times,* March 2, 2017, available at https://www.nytimes.com/2017/03/02/world/europe/sweden-draft-conscription.html?_r=0.

[4] Russian Foreign Minister Sergei Lavrov, quoted in, Hui Min Neo, Bryan McManus, "U.S. Pledges 'Unwavering' Commitment, Europe Lukewarm," AFP, February 18, 2017, at https://www.yahoo.com/news/pence-caps-week-us-diplomatic-efforts-calm-allies-0558127929.html.

[5] Then-Commander of the United States European Command, Gen. Philip Breedlove, said in Feb. 2016, "Russia's continued aggressive actions and malign influence remain a top concern for our nation and my highest priority as EUCOM Commander." General Philip Breedlove, Commander, United States European Command, United States European Command Posture Statement 2016, February 25, 2016, at http://www.eucom.mil/media-library/article/35164/u-s-european-command-posture-statement-2016.

[6] See for example, Keith Payne and John Foster, *Russian Strategy: Expansion, Crisis and Conflict* (Fairfax, VA: National Institute Press, 2016). See also, Dave Johnson, "Nuclear Weapons in Russia's Approach to Conflict," *Recherches & Documents,* No. 6 (November 2016), p.13, at, www.FRSTRATEGIE.org.

[7] Reported in, Michael Gordon, "Russian Cruise Missile, Deployed Secretly, Violates Treaty, Officials Say," *The New York Times,* February 14, 2017, at, https://www.nytimes.com/2017/02/14/world.europe/russia-cruise-missile-rms-control-treaty.html?rref=collection%2Fbyline%2F_michael-r.-gordon. See also, Adm. Harry Harris, Commander, U.S. Pacific Command, *The View from the Indo-Asia-Pacific,* WEST 2017 Conference Lunch Keynote, San Diego, CA, February 21, 2017, p. 4, available at, http://www.pacom.mil/Meida/Speeches-Testimony/Article/1089966/west-2017-keynote-the-view-from-the-indo-asia-pacific/.

[8] "Russia today is not interested in U.S.-proposed arms reduction—Sergei Ivanov," *Interfax,* March 5, 2013. (Transcribed by World News Connection).

[9] The Commander of U.S. Strategic Command, Gen. John Hyten, has rightly described U.S. strategic nuclear forces: "All our stuff is old. It's still ready, safe, secure, reliable. It's old." See, "Hyten: Modernize, Don't Increase Number of Nukes," *Air Force Magazine,* March 2, 2017, available at http://airforcemag.com/DRArchive/Pages/2017/March%202017/March%2002%202017/Hyten-Modernize,-Don't-Increase-Number-of-Nukes.aspx.

Russia's coercive nuclear threats and reported planning for nuclear first use presents a profound new challenge for Western deterrence and assurance strategies. [10] This is not speculation about some dark future; this challenge is here and now. [11] In response, some European officials, including in Germany, reportedly now are discussing an independent nuclear "Euro-deterrent," [12] and NATO's Deputy Supreme Allied Commander, Sir Adrian Bradshaw, describes the current threat context in stark terms: "The threat from Russia is that through opportunism and mistakes and a lack of clarity regarding our deterrence we find ourselves sliding into an unwanted conflict which has existential implications." [13]

Consequently, priority goals for the forthcoming United States Nuclear Posture Review must be to: 1) understand Russian goals and strategy; 2) understand why Moscow believes it has exploitable advantages that now enable it to change the post-Cold War order and issue coercive nuclear first-use threats, and; 3) identify in light of those goals and beliefs how the West can effectively deter Moscow and assure allies. I will take just a few minutes to address these questions.

First, based on open Russian writings and speeches over years, it is clear that Moscow is driven to correct what it perceives to be the geopolitical injustices of the post-Cold War order forced on it by the West in Russia's time of weakness. President Putin famously called the collapse of the Soviet Union the greatest catastrophe of the Twentieth Century. [14]

The West supposedly has pushed Russia too far and has further highly-aggressive designs against Russia, including regime change. Consequently, the Putin regime is rearming Russia and changing European borders with the expressed goal of overturning the despised post-Cold War settlement and restoring Russia's power position. This combination of Russian goals and perceptions make friction with the West inevitable: it carries the potential for high stakes conflict and even nuclear escalation.

Further, Russia believes it has the capability and the will to overturn the status-quo, while it doubts NATO's resolve to resist *if Russia poses the threat of war and nuclear coercion.* Moscow's self-image, in addition to its skepticism regarding NATO's resolve threaten deterrence in Europe and understandably frightens our allies.

I am *not* suggesting here that Russia wants war or is cavalier about the prospect of nuclear war. However, Moscow's perception of an asymmetry in resolve and readiness to risk war is key to the potential for deterrence failure in Europe and the need to assure threatened allies.

In short, Russia appears to have some felt-freedom to move against the West given its perception of this asymmetry of need, will and power. Just how much freedom Russia believes it has to expand its position and how it will act with that freedom likely depends on Moscow's calculations of NATO's determination, readiness and power to resist. That is a calculation the West can affect by its statements and actions.

For example, some commentators assert that the Putin regime has dangerous designs on the Baltic states, others say it has no such designs. My point is that there probably is not a fixed answer to this question regarding Russia's readiness to act

---

[10] There are many open discussions regarding allied concerns. See for example, Bradley Peniston, "A Key NATO Ally Looks Nervously at Putin—And Trump," *Defense One,* January 23, 2017, at http://www.defenseone.com/threats/2017/01/key-nato-ally-looks-nervously-putin-and-trump/134765/.

[11] Given these unfortunate realities, key Obama administration officials rightly concluded that we are now playing catch-up as the modernization of U.S. nuclear capabilities is priority number one for the deterrence of enemies and the assurance of allies. As a 2016 DOD report states: "The nuclear deterrent is the DOD's highest priority mission," Department of Defense, Office of the Assistant Secretary of Defense for Nuclear, Chemical, and Biological Defense Programs, *Strategic Planning Guidance FY 2018–2022,* February 2016, p. 2. As former Secretary of Defense Carter noted in November 2016, "While we didn't build anything new for 25 years, and neither did our allies, others did—including Russia, North Korea, China, Pakistan, India, and for a period of time, Iran. We [now] can't wait any longer."Quoted in, Jamie McIntyre, "Carter Says Nuclear-Armed Foes Catching Up to the U.S.," *Washington Examiner,* November 3, 2016, at http://www.washingtonexaminer.com/carter-says-nuclear-armed-foes-catching-up-to-the-us/article/2606380.

[12] Max Fisher, "Fearing U.S. Withdrawal, Europe Considers Its Own Nuclear Deterrent," *The New York Times,* March 6, 2017, available at https://www.nytimes.com/2017/03/06/world/europe/european-union-nuclear-weapons.html.

[13] Sam Jones, "Nato and EU need 'grand strategy' to resist Putin, says general," *Financial Times,* March 2, 2017, available at https://www.ft.com/content/e8dc5f7c-ff67–11e6–8d8e-a5e3738f9ae4.

[14] Andrew Osborn, "Putin: Collapse of the Soviet Union was 'catastrophe of the century,'" *The Independent,* April 26, 2005, available at http://www.independent.co.uk/news/world/europe/putin-collapse-of-the-soviet-union-was-catastrophe-of-the-century-521064.html.

on its aspirations and perceptions of advantage. Rather the Putin regime is pragmatic and the West can act to limit Moscow's agenda and actions vis-à-vis the Baltic states and elsewhere. This possible constraint on Moscow is what makes Russia today different from Germany of the late 1930s, and why strengthening NATO's deterrence position is so critical.

What are the implications of these realities for Western deterrence and assurance strategies and requirements? The most basic need is for U.S. policies and forces that are of sufficient size and flexibility to adapt as necessary to an increasingly hostile and dynamic nuclear threat environment.[15] That principle alone is very different from the previous dominant post-Cold War policy direction which sought largely to reduce and constrain U.S. nuclear capabilities on a continuing basis.

More specifically, the West must end Russian misperceptions that Moscow's will and readiness to break the West at the risk of war are greater than the West's will and readiness to prevent it from doing so.

We can help in this regard with consistent, resolute alliance-wide declaratory policies, along with relevant exercises, that signal a message of resolve to Moscow that the United States and NATO will not prove wobbly, even *under Moscow's coercive nuclear threats,* i.e., the West must deny Moscow any expectation of an exploitable advantage in political will.

A useful example of a helpful declaratory policy was provided in 2016 by the then-new British Prime Minister, Theresa May. When asked in Parliament if she would ever authorize a nuclear strike given the dangers involved, she responded yes without hesitation. Prime Minister May added, "The whole point of a deterrent is that our enemies need to know that we would be prepared to use it ... We must send an unequivocal message to any adversary that the cost of an attack on our United Kingdom or our allies will be far greater than anything it might hope to gain."[16] No doubt Moscow paid considerable attention to that unambiguous deterrence signal.

A related theme in Russian writings is Moscow's apparent belief that Russia has exploitable nuclear and conventional force advantages over the West. These include greater, immediately-available local conventional force capabilities and readiness. President Putin has boasted that he can have Russian troops in five NATO capitals in two days.[17] These perceived advantages also include Russian nuclear escalation options to which NATO is thought to have no response given Russian skepticism about the West's will to resist.

The interaction here between increased Western non-nuclear defense preparedness in Europe and the perceived credibility of the West's nuclear deterrent is important. In response to Russian threats and expansionism, Western efforts to deploy high-readiness, *non-nuclear* defensive capabilities to protect NATO front-line states from a Russian military fait accompli will likely reduce Moscow's perceptions of exploitable advantage and also strengthen the credibility of U.S. extended deterrence commitments. Why? Because doing so will deny Moscow's perceptions of an easy Russian fait accompli and demonstrate united Western resolve to put itself on the line for this cause. The West understood this point well during the Cold War. To use Cold War terms, a conventional "plate glass door" that is understood by Moscow to lead to intolerable loss if it should attack can be of great value for deterrence.

The level of additional, forward-deployed NATO defensive capability needed for this deterrent purpose is an important question. Lt. Gen. Valery Zaparenko, a former deputy chief of the Russian General Staff commented recently in this regard, "You can't deter much with a few battalions."[18] A pertinent 2016 RAND study concluded that: "Having a force of about seven brigades, including three heavy armored brigades—adequately supported by airpower, land-based fires, and other enablers on

[15] This need for adaptability has been emphasized by the Trump Administration's National Security Advisor, Lt. Gen. H.R. McMaster. See, *Strategy, Policy and History,* Lieutenant General H.R. McMaster, U.S. Army, Moderator: Dr. Mark Moyar, Foreign Policy Initiative, FPI Forum Transcript, November 20, 2016, p. 10.

[16] Theresa May, as quoted in House of Commons Hansard, "UK's Nuclear Deterrent," *Parliament.uk,* July 18, 2016, available at https://hansard.parliament.uk/Commons/2016–07–18/debates/16071818000001/UKSNuclearDeterrent?highlight=Care.

[17] Quoted in, Justin Huggler, "Putin 'privately threatened to invade Poland, Romania and the Baltic states,'" *The Telegraph,* September 18, 2014, available at http://www.telegraph.co.uk/news/worldnews/europe/russia/11106195/Putin-privately-threatened-to-invade-Poland-Romania-and-the-Baltic-states.html.

[18] Matthew Bodner, "No End In Sight for Russia's Baltic Tit-for-Tat," *The Moscow Times,* September 23, 2016, available at https://themoscowtimes.com/articles/baltic-tit-for-tat-55434.

the ground and ready to fight at the onset of hostilities" might provide an adequate initial deterrent.[19]

The difference today, of course, is that NATO front-line states are former parts of the Soviet Union or former members of its Warsaw Pact. This point may be extremely significant because cognitive studies typically conclude that humans will accept greater risk to recover a value considered unfairly lost than to acquire a new gain. The leadership in Moscow clearly believes the West has inflicted great losses on Russia that must be recovered. This point suggests the challenge of deterring the Russian leadership in this second nuclear age; our Cold War approaches to deterrence are incomplete guides for contemporary deterrence strategies.

Because Moscow views nuclear escalation as an exploitable threat or act—based in part on its perceived ability to control escalation to its advantage—the West's deterrence and assurance strategies can neither escape the nuclear dimension nor be limited to in-theater capabilities. There are no solely non-nuclear or wholly local fixes that can fully address NATO's deterrence needs.

Some Western steps in this regard include:

- Modernizing the U.S. nuclear triad, to include some very low-yield options on accurate U.S. strategic missile systems,[20] and strengthening command and control systems;
- Deploying U.S. national missile defense capabilities sufficient to deny any opponent a plausible strategy of coercing Washington via threats of limited nuclear attack[21] (this step also is essential given the emerging North Korean ICBM threat to the United States);[22]
- Advancing the delivery date of the nuclear-capable F–35 and B61–12 combination;[23]
- Retaining the unique capabilities of the B61–11;
- Increasing NATO DCA survivability and readiness;[24]
- Expanding DCA burden sharing, possibly by inviting personnel from additional NATO states to serve as DCA pilots;
- Ensuring that NATO conventional forces can survive and fight in the context of limited Russian nuclear escalation;
- Increasing the active and passive defense of key NATO nodes and assets against conventional and nuclear strike; and,
- Ensuring the capability to penetrate advanced defensive systems such as the S–500.

Finally, the development of "new" U.S. nuclear capabilities should not be ruled out peremptorily by policy.[25] Increased United States nuclear force numbers may well be *unnecessary,* but there are some plausible capabilities that could help reduce

---

[19] David A. Shlapak and Michael W. Johnson, *Reinforcing Deterrence on NATO's Eastern Flank: Wargaming the Defense of the Baltics* (Washington, D.C.: RAND Corporation, 2016), p. 1, available at https://www.rand.org/content/dam/rand/pubs/research_reports/RR1200/RR1253/RAND_RR1253.pdf.

[20] Defense Science Board, *Seven Defense Priorities for the New Administration* (Washington, D.C.: Defense Science Board, December 2016), p. 24, available at http://www.acq.osd.mil/dsb/reports/Seven_Defense_Priorities.pdf.

[21] Tom Karako, Keith Payne, Brad Roberts, et. al., *Defense and Defeat: A Report of the CSIS Missile Defense Project* (New York: Rowman & Littlefield, March 2017), available at https://csis-prod.s3.amazonaws.com/s3fs-public/publication/170228_Karako_MissileDefenseDefeat_Web.pdf?.oYEfXIARU6HCqtRN3Zuq7mKljU3jIlq.

[22] The Chairman of the JCS, Gen. Joseph Dunford, recently observed, "Clearly we see now a combination of both intercontinental ballistic missile capability as well as an effort to put a nuclear warhead on that intercontinental ballistic missile. North Korea not only threatens South Korea and not only threaten the region but now presents a threat to the Homeland as well." Dunford Speaks at Brookings Institution," *Department of Defense,* February 23, 2017, available at https://www.defense.gov/Video?videoid=511122.

[23] See Orianna Pawlyk, "F–35 Could Carry B61 Nuclear Warhead Sooner Than Planned," *Tech,* January 10, 2017, at, http://defensetech.org/2017/01/10/f-35-carry-b61-nuclear-warhead-sooner-planned/.

[24] A December 2015 NATO report states that DCA aircraft, "are available for nuclear roles at various levels of readiness—the highest level of readiness is measured in weeks." An earlier GAO Report to Congress places that time at 30 days. See respectively, *NATO's Nuclear Deterrence Policy and Forces,* December 3, 2015, available at, http://www.nato.int/cps/en/natohq/topics_50068.html; and GAO, Report to Congressional Requesters, *Nuclear Weapons: DOD and NNSA Need to Better Manage Scope of Future Refurbishments and Risks to Maintaining U.S. Commitments to NATO,* GAO–11–387, May 2011, p. 5.

[25] Defense Science Board, *Seven Defense Priorities for the New Administration,* op. cit. See also the comments by Air Force Chief of Staff, Gen. David Goldfein, in "Nuclear Posture Review Due in Spring: Air Force Chief," *Exchange Monitor,* February 9, 2017, available at http://www.exchangemonitor.com/publication/morning-briefing/nuclear-posture-review-due-spring-air-force-chief/.

Moscow's perceptions of exploitable advantages. It should be recalled that then-Commander of STRATCOM, General Kevin Chilton, observed publicly that the United States nuclear force posture deemed adequate for the 2010 NPR was predicated on the assumptions that Russia would abide by its arms control treaty commitments, and that there would be no call for additional capabilities.[26] The Russians have since violated the former assumption, and the latter is now an open question given Moscow's expansionism, buildup of new nuclear forces, and dangerous views of escalation.

The fiscal year 2016 NDAA's discussion of the U.S. Stockpile Responsiveness Program indicates that there is bipartisan support for, " ... the policy of the United States to identify, sustain, enhance, integrate, and continually exercise all capabilities required to conceptualize, study, design, develop, engineer, certify, produce, and deploy nuclear weapons to ensure the nuclear deterrent of the United States remains safe, secure, reliable, credible, and responsive."[27] Nevertheless, some commentators suggest that any "new" U.S. nuclear capability would likely upset the delicate domestic political consensus in favor of U.S. nuclear modernization, and thus must be rejected.[28] This domestic political concern may be valid and an important consideration, but any review of emerging policy and force needs should at least identify those steps that could serve to strengthen deterrence and assurance—even if a subsequent political decision is made to avoid such steps given anticipated domestic political costs. The prospective trade-offs of such a decision must be understood.

However that question is resolved, a more robust and unified Western declaratory policy should complement any new steps. The long-held policy notion that uncertainty and ambiguity with regard to Western deterrence strategy is adequate for deterrence needs to be reconsidered. The historical evidence is overwhelming that uncertainty and ambiguity sometimes are not adequate for deterrence. Rather, explicit and direct deterrence statements are necessary in some cases. As former Defense Secretary Leon Panetta recently observed, in some cases credible deterrence demands that the United States "make it very clear" that "we will respond in kind."[29] Effective deterrence of the Putin regime may be such a case.

There is much more to say about these critical questions of post-Cold War deterrence and assurance, but I will stop at this point to stay within my allotted time. I look forward to your questions.

Senator FISCHER. Thank you, Dr. Payne.

Dr. Samore, welcome.

STATEMENT OF DR. GARY S. SAMORE, EXECUTIVE DIRECTOR FOR RESEARCH, BELFER CENTER FOR SCIENCE AND INTERNATIONAL AFFAIRS, HARVARD KENNEDY SCHOOL

Dr. SAMORE. Thank you, Madam Chair. Thank you, Senator Donnelly. I want to thank the subcommittee for giving me this opportunity to talk about the emerging nuclear context.

The first thing I want to say is that in my view the basic nuclear landscape is not likely to change dramatically in the next five to ten years in terms of the number of countries that possess nuclear weapons. As you all know, nine countries have nuclear weapons—the United States, Russia, China, U.K., France, India, Pakistan, Israel and North Korea—and all of those countries view nuclear weapons as essential to their defense and their foreign policy objectives. None of them are prepared to give them up, and all of them will take the necessary steps to maintain, modernize, and expand

---

[26] Kevin Chilton, as quoted in, "Nuclear Posture Review," 111th U.S. Congress, Senate Armed Services Committee, April 22, 2010, available at https://www.gpo.gov/fdsys/pkg/CHRG–111shrg63689/html/CHRG–111shrg63689.htm

[27] Fiscal year 2016 NDAA, Sec. 4220(a), enacted December 23, 2016.

[28] James Acton, "Policy Outlook Panel," Nuclear Deterrence Summit, Washington, D.C., February 28, 2017.

[29] Brian Everstine, "Thornberry: Expect Nuclear Tests During the Lame Duck," *Air Force Magazine,* December 2, 2016, available at http://www.airforcemag.com/DRArchive/Pages/2016/December%202016/December%2002%202016/Thornberry-Expect-Nuclear-Tests-During-the-Lame-Duck.aspx.

their nuclear forces in order to meet their interests. In other words, we're not likely to see any significant move toward nuclear disarmament in that time period.

At the same time, I think the number of additional countries seeking to acquire nuclear weapons is very limited. The focus, of course, is on Iran. If the current nuclear agreement remains in force, then Iran's ability to develop nuclear weapons is constrained for at least 10 to 15 years.

Beyond Iran, the proliferation risk is really limited to the Middle East, countries that feel directly threatened by Iran like Turkey and Saudi Arabia, and the Far East, countries like Japan and South Korea that feel directly threatened by North Korea.

In all of these cases, I think there are a combination of technical constraints and political constraints that give us a good ability, give us good policy tools to prevent those countries, which are friends and allies and partners of the United States, from developing their own nuclear weapons, in particular if we maintain our strong security ties and extended deterrence with respect to those countries.

In terms of direct nuclear threats to the United States, Russia and China will obviously remain the dominant existential threats over the next five to ten years. Both Russia and China will continue to modernize their nuclear forces, especially in terms of deploying a new generation of submarines and road-mobilized ICBMs in order to assure a survivable nuclear force that can overcome U.S. missile defense capabilities and, from their standpoint, have an assured ability to inflict unacceptable damage.

Assuming the United States proceeds with its own modernization program, neither Russia nor China will be able to achieve any option to attack the United States without being destroyed themselves. In other words, I think the nuclear balance between the United States and Russia and between the United States and China is likely to remain robust over the next five to ten years.

In terms of arms control, the New START Treaty helps to maintain strategic stability between the United States and Russia in terms of imposing verifiable limits on deployed strategic warheads and delivery vehicles, but I doubt we'll see any dramatic breakthroughs in bilateral arms control for the time being.

In particular, Russia will not accept additional limits on its offensive forces unless the United States accepts quantitative and qualitative limits on missile defense, and I don't think we can do that because of emerging threats, in particular North Korea.

At the same time, I think Moscow will want to keep the New START Treaty in place and probably extend it because it provides reliability and transparency.

The INF Treaty, which Russia has violated by deploying prohibitive ground-launched cruise missiles, is probably unsalvageable, but the strategic consequences are modest.

Finally, in terms of new nuclear threats on the horizon, North Korea's program to develop a nuclear-armed ICBM is clearly the most significant and the most immediate. I think it's difficult to calculate or predict when North Korea might achieve that capability, a reliable nuclear-armed ICBM, but certainly with the pace of testing they've been carrying out, something in the next five to ten years seems like a reasonable guess.

Unfortunately, our ability to prevent North Korea from achieving that capability with military or diplomatic tools is very limited, although we might be able to delay the program. In the end, I think deterrence and missile defense is probably going to be our most effective response.

The bottom line, nuclear weapons will remain an enduring feature of the international security landscape and U.S. defense for the foreseeable future. As a result, I think we'll need to maintain and modernize our nuclear forces, as the other two witnesses have said. We can debate details and numbers, schedules and particular weapons systems, but having a robust and effective nuclear force is likely to be important for the foreseeable future.

Thank you, Madam Chair.

Senator FISCHER. Thank you.

I know that all of you have mentioned this explicitly or implied it in your testimony, but I would ask you to respond to these questions.

In 2010 the NPR stated, "Retaining all three triad legs will best maintain strategic stability at a reasonable cost while hedging against potential technical problems or vulnerabilities." Do each of you believe this statement remains accurate and that the new NPR should validate the triad's lasting importance?

Dr. SAMORE. Yes.

Dr. PAYNE. Yes.

General KEHLER. Yes.

Senator FISCHER. Thank you. Do you all believe the NPR should also validate the current modernization plans?

Dr. Samore?

Dr. SAMORE. As I said, I think there's room for debate about schedules and deadlines and particular weapons systems and numbers, and this is mainly because of budgetary considerations. I mean, it's going to be a very expensive modernization program, and I think it would be legitimate for Congress to take a look at that program and see whether or not Congress wants to tinker with the cost by extending deadlines, reducing numbers and so forth.

I don't have a particular view about that, but my point is that I think that there's a lot of flexibility, or there's at least some flexibility in that program which one might want to employ for reasons of saving some money.

Senator FISCHER. If the budget constraints were not an issue, would you change your answer?

Dr. SAMORE. No. I think the only hesitation I have is because of budgetary issues.

Senator FISCHER. Okay, thank you.

Dr. Payne?

Dr. PAYNE. I think getting on with the modernization plan of record, with the schedule that's now there, is important, and I certainly think that the NPR should endorse that.

Senator FISCHER. General Kehler?

General KEHLER. Madam Chair, given the conditions, if the budget was not a constraint, I would want to accelerate some things, actually. I support the program as it's been laid out.

Senator FISCHER. Okay, thank you.

In his 2011 message to the Senate on the New START Treaty, President Obama promised to accelerate the design and construction of the plutonium and uranium facilities within the Department of Energy's nuclear enterprise, and for a variety of reasons these facilities remain incomplete.

Do each of you believe that the country requires a responsive nuclear enterprise, including in plutonium and uranium facilities, and that the new NPR should confirm this need?

Dr. SAMORE. Yes.

Dr. PAYNE. Yes.

General KEHLER. Yes.

Senator FISCHER. Very good. Okay. This is easy, isn't it?

General Kehler, given your experience as a former STRATCOM commander, can you speak to the value of an air-launched cruise missile, the value that that provides, and your thoughts on the importance of the [Long Range Standoff Weapon] LRSO program?

General KEHLER. Madam Chair, we have well over 30 years of experience now with long-range missiles associated with bombers, and what we found both in a conventional sense where we've used them in combat many, many, many times over the intervening years, and certainly in the value that they have played for deterrence, I fully support the requirement to have a long-range missile associated with our bomber force. It allows us to take a standoff platform like the B–52 and keep it viable, and it takes a penetrating platform like the B–21 and makes it more lethal.

In both of those cases, this is not incompatible. I do think the LRSO has a bad name, actually, because it isn't necessarily a long-range standoff weapon. The questions that I've gotten about this have been why does a penetrating bomber need a standoff weapon? It's really misnamed. We've had long-range missiles associated with penetrating bombers back to the B–52. When the B–52 used to penetrate, it also had long-range missiles on it.

To me, this is not incompatible. It's about viability of a platform like the B–52 in a standoff role, and it's about lethality of a penetrating bomber that allows us to cover a greater part of the target base, hold that at risk, and ultimately enhance deterrence.

Senator FISCHER. Thank you.

The Obama Administration, like its predecessors, considered taking the U.S. ICBMs off alert and rejected that policy, maintaining the current alert posture.

General Kehler, do you believe any changes should be made to the current alert posture?

General KEHLER. I do not. In my view, as long as a nuclear-armed adversary has the ability to strike us quickly, we should retain the capability to respond quickly. The issues about hair triggers are typically about use-or-lose and concerns about vulnerability. As I said before, this is not the Cold War. That situation doesn't look quite the same as it did in the Cold War. That would require a massive attack from the Russians. No one else can do that besides the Russians. The Chinese can't do that. It's really about making sure that we have taken steps both to plan around a use-or-lose kind of scenario. If you think about this, the plans for New START will eventually have the bulk of our weapons aboard submarines. It's also about—not about the trigger, it's about the trigger finger, and it's about making sure that the decision-maker has decision time. A lot of work has been done to extend the amount of decision time associated with those kinds of decisions that might come with time urgency associated with them.

I think this problem looks different today than it did in the Cold War. I think that we get tremendous deterrent value out of having the ability to respond quickly. An attacker would have to take that into account. I think that in the context of the triad, I believe that retaining ICBMs in a ready-to-use posture is the right way to go, especially since they're aimed at broad ocean areas.

Senator FISCHER. Thank you, sir.

I would ask all of you, do you believe that the United States forces are adequately configured to respond to Russia's deescalate strategy in the event that the deterrence would fail? What additional steps should we be considering to, I guess, better dissuade Russia from continuing down that road?

Dr. Samore?

Dr. SAMORE. I think the most important way to prevent the Russians from employing that strategy is a very strong conventional defense in NATO. I think the steps that have been taken since the Russian seizure of Crimea and the invasion of Ukraine are important steps. I think we should take a look at other things we need to do, in particular to defend the Baltic states, so the Russians understand that any conventional aggression against those countries would mean war against NATO.

We don't want to find ourselves in a situation where the Russians have invaded the Baltic states, we're in a conflict with them and they use low-yield nuclear weapons, which are very important to them, much more important to them than they are to us in terms of our overall defense strategy.

I think deterrence is the name of the game here. We don't want to be responding to a Russian use of nuclear weapons in Europe. If they were to do that, yes, I think we have sufficient forces to respond.

Senator FISCHER. Thank you.

Dr. Payne?

Dr. PAYNE. I would only add to what Gary said, that increasing the NATO DCA survivability and readiness would be an important step. Right now, according to open sources, the highest level alert for NATO DC aircraft is several weeks. My guess is—in fact, I'm sure that making that much better—I don't know if we'll need to go back to quick action alert status of the Cold War, but doing much better than a couple of weeks or weeks for our readiness would be extremely important to help discourage Moscow from thinking that it can engage in a limited nuclear strike.

Senator FISCHER. Thank you, sir.

General Kehler?

General KEHLER. I agree with both of my colleagues. I would only add a couple of points.

One is I think this says something about the wisdom of keeping U.S. weapons in Europe committed to the NATO alliance. I would make sure that the B–61 life extension program is funded and that we are watching that very carefully to make sure that that's proceeding apace.

The second thing I would do is I would look carefully at the plans for the F–35 and its deployment and nuclear certification, when that is supposed to happen and when maybe we ought to have that happen. We might want to do something different there. I don't know that for sure, but that's something for us to think about.

The other thing we ought to at least have on our plate is how this might shape the future of missile defenses in Europe.

Senator FISCHER. Thank you very much.

Senator Donnelly?

Senator DONNELLY. Thank you, Madam Chair.

Dr. Samore, you mentioned about low yield being important to the Russians. Do you believe that our capabilities can also match on the low yield end, if necessary?

Dr. SAMORE. I think that the B–61 gives us a flexible response and will allow us to use nuclear weapons in Europe in that scenario. Again, we don't want to be confronted with a situation in Europe where tactical nuclear weapons are being used. I'm very skeptical that that can be controlled. I think there would be extremely high risk that that would escalate to general nuclear conflict. The name of the game here is to prevent a war in Europe, and I think conventional deterrence is the most important line of defense.

I think, as my colleagues have suggested, I would look at things to do to strengthen our conventional capability. I don't particularly see any need for us to develop a new low-yield weapon, but I'm open to it. If NATO military experts study the issue and believe, especially in light of Russian violation of the INF Treaty, we need new systems for military purposes, then I think that's something we should do, and I don't myself see any immediate requirement for it.

Senator DONNELLY. General Kehler, do you believe that we have the ability in the low-yield area at the present time?

General KEHLER. I would agree with Dr. Samore on this one. I think that one of the features of the modernization plans that have been laid out is retaining an ability to hedge our bets here. I think the B–61 does give us quite a bit of capability here, especially the life-extended B–61. I think that that gives us something at the lower-yield end here.

I would also agree, though, if in studying this and watching what's happening with the Russians a need arises, then we ought to be in a position to field something that's of lower yield. That says to me that what we have to do is make sure that the weapons complex can handle that kind of task if it's given to them. That gets back to the features of investing in the infrastructure to make sure that the weapons complex could do that if and when it becomes necessary.

Senator DONNELLY. General, do you believe, when you hear about the Russians talking about a low-yield strategy, escalate to deescalate, do you think, in the experience you've had, that Vladimir Putin believes that, or is he rattling sabers, that that is a viable strategy?

General KEHLER. Senator, that's the $64,000 question. I don't know. The way I was always taught to think about deterrence was there are two ways that you look at an adversary: one is capability; the other is intent. Capability doesn't change quickly; intent does. All I can go on is what they say publicly, and then watch carefully about what their capabilities are. In this case, it looks like they are wanting to deploy some capabilities that would back that up. That would concern me if I was still wearing a uniform because I don't know what their intent really is, but if they have the capability to do something, that would worry me.

I also believe, though, like my colleagues, this is very dangerous ground for them to be on, and I think that—you know, a predecessor of mine some years ago said something that stuck with me. All this theory, thankfully, has never been tested. I think one of the issues here is the risk that goes with nuclear matters writ large. It's why they have deterrent value, by the way. I think there's tremendous risk here in the way the Russians are talking about their weapons.

Senator DONNELLY. In other words, take him at his word and prepare for it.

General KEHLER. As a military person, I couldn't do that any other way, actually.

Senator DONNELLY. Dr. Payne?

Dr. PAYNE. We're reading tea leaves, like back in the Cold War when the Sovietologists tried to figure out who was thinking what.

My view, and I would look at this very seriously, is that the Putin regime writ large does have some confidence in its escalate-to-deescalate approach. You can see that this approach goes back to its exercises, back to ZAPAD–99, where according to open sources it used four cruise missiles, and after it used four nuclear-armed cruise missiles the West stopped.

What you see are exercises that look like they're reflecting escalate-to-deescalate. I read the Russian military daily. The Russian military talks about escalate-to-deescalate in very precise terms. It looks like the exercises go along those ways. It looks like they're developing forces exactly for that and have developed forces for that. On that basis I have to conclude, with General Kehler, that to prepare for something more benign than that would be imprudent.

Senator DONNELLY. General, do you believe it's in the national security interest of the United States to continue implementation of the New START Treaty? If so, why?

General KEHLER. I do. I took command at STRATCOM right after the New START was ratified. My predecessor was asked if he supported it; he did. I was asked that subsequent to that. I supported it as well. I still support it. I think that we have gotten tremendous benefit out of those kinds of agreements with the Russians over the years, provided that the Russians comply. It looks to me—and again, all I see is what's publicly available today—that our benefit here in terms of on-site inspections, in terms of data exchanges, in terms of the very interchanges that are required to execute these agreements provide value to us. I also think that it has reduced the threat that we have to face.

I believe for a long time that there are two ways to reduce the threat. One is by reducing the weapons, and the other is by deterring the remainder.

Senator DONNELLY. Dr. Payne, I wanted to ask you a little bit about North Korea's KNOA. In focusing on a low-yield capability, as you look at this it seems that the challenge—the primary issue may not be so much targeting it but finding it. Do you think that a strategy involving a conventional strike capability which could destroy it has the advantage of leveraging significant investments we've already made? Do you think that's a sufficient strategy or not?

Dr. PAYNE. I think it's necessary but not sufficient, necessary but insufficient. I would like to see that, but in addition strengthening U.S. missile defense capabilities, particularly near term for Hawaii, for example, which may be one of the most near-term targets that the North Koreans could reach, and there are ways we could do that that I think are relatively inexpensive, largely with the assets we have now. I'd like to see a combination of both offensive options but also defensive options just in case the offensive options aren't available or are seen as too provocative at the time.

Senator DONNELLY. Thank you.

Thank you, Madam Chair.

Senator FISCHER. Senator Inhofe?

Senator INHOFE. Thank you, Madam Chair.

You know, when you're out away from Washington and around real people and you remind them that we have reduced our capability since the Cold War by 70 percent or something like that, while other countries, the obvious ones—China, Russia, and others—it was pointed out, as Dr. Samore has said, some nine different countries have been increasing theirs, it's a real shock treatment to them because they look at that as our vulnerability.

Now, I would first of all just ask you, is it a lack of priority by not just the last administration but going back to the Clinton Administration, that we have not put our emphasis on this deterrent? Back when you had your uniform on, how would you have answered that at that time?

General KEHLER. Sir, I think it's a combination of a lot of reasons. One, when the Cold War ended, there was a sense I think that we had crossed some line that perhaps we didn't need these weapons in quite the same way that we needed them in the Cold War. I think certainly the conventional conflicts that we got engaged in, certainly after 9/11 I think had, from my observation anyway, a lot to do with the focus that we placed on the nuclear deterrent. I think we put all of that, to use an Air Force term, on autopilot, and I think over time we had benign neglect. As a result of that, we now find ourselves in a time when there's a sense of urgency that has to go with recapitalizing this.

Senator INHOFE. Well, yes. Now has your thinking changed, since we now are looking at North Korea where its leadership are somewhat mentally defective, totally unpredictable? Does that change your thinking in terms of priorities?

General KEHLER. It does, and that's why I think you will have some very difficult priority decisions to make in any budget that comes forward, I'm sure. I think modernizing and recapitalizing the nuclear deterrent and its supporting elements needs to go to the top of that priority list. I think now is the time.

Senator INHOFE. Okay. Dr. Samore, without your notes you quickly responded as to the nine countries. Give us the top four in terms of your concern, of your list of nine.

Dr. SAMORE. Well, the top three that directly threaten the United States are Russia, China, and North Korea. The other countries have nuclear weapons for their defense, but it's hard to imagine a situation in which they would directly threaten the United States.

Senator INHOFE. The third one you mentioned, North Korea, that's the one that's unpredictable. Doesn't that in some ways concern you more?

Dr. SAMORE. It's very unpredictable. As a consequence I think missile defense has to be developed in order to ensure that we can protect ourselves against that North Korean threat.

Senator INHOFE. Okay. Now, on modernization, are we looking at capabilities, or are we looking at safety? The reason I ask that, a very prominent former war fighter told me a few minutes ago that back when a lightning strike might have come carrying a weapon, that could have activated it, and now some of the modernization has made that safer so that they're not carrying around something that could be activated, or even deployed.

Is safety a major area that we have been sacrificing by allowing other countries to progress further than we are?

Dr. SAMORE. Well, others may be better equipped to answer that than I am. My impression is that our current nuclear weapons are extremely safe. I think modernization is really more a question of developing new delivery systems——

Senator INHOFE. I apologize because I was directing that to General Kehler.

Dr. SAMORE. Oh, I'm sorry.

General KEHLER. Sorry. This is almost like choosing between the children, because I am not concerned that our weapons would be hard to use if they needed to be used. I am concerned that security is different today than it was when these weapons were designed and fielded for the Cold War.

Insider threats, for example, other things that we see every day in the news in other places, cyber threats, I think we need to take those very, very seriously, and we need to be sure that we have done everything we need to do to address whatever concerns we find in those regards. Safety is the same kind of thing where I don't think you can separate that.

I don't believe there's an issue today with the ability for the United States to use those weapons if so ordered.

Senator INHOFE. Okay. Dr. Payne, a few minutes ago you made the statement—I didn't get the rest of your statement. You said we need to look carefully at the F–35. In what context was it that you made that statement a minute ago?

Dr. PAYNE. Well, I'd very much like to see the nuclear-capable F–35 and the B61–12 combination advanced to an earlier entry date, if that's possible, and there's some evidence that it's possible.

Senator INHOFE. Okay, good. Well, that is significant. Some don't agree with that.

The last question I'd have for you, General Kehler. In your opening statement you made a comment. About two years ago you took your uniform off, so you have some different ideas now than you had at that time, or different priorities. What do you see differently now that your uniform is off than you did at that time?

General KEHLER. Senator, I actually don't have a different view about the way forward than I did then. I am certainly more concerned. The United States hadn't slapped the table about an INF violation by the time I left that was about to happen but it hadn't happened yet. That concerns me.

The plans that are in front of you today I had a hand in shaping, both as a member of the Nuclear Weapons Council and as the Commander of Strategic Command. I had a hand in shaping the policies that are sitting there in front of you today, the nuclear employment strategy that's sitting in front of you today, and by and large I still support that range of things that were put in place.

Senator INHOFE. Thank you, Madam Chair.

Senator FISCHER. Thank you, Senator.

Senator Heinrich?

Senator HEINRICH. General Kehler, congratulations on the liberty that your uniform provides for this setting. I want to go back to New START for a second. New START allows the United States to conduct 18 on-site inspections of Russian strategic nuclear forces each year, and we've done that, I believe, every year since the treaty was signed.

In addition, the treaty maintains an extensive database and mandates unique identifiers of Russia's strategic forces.

What are some of the benefits of, in particular the intelligence benefits, of having inspections and database and unique identifiers? What would be the implications if we were to lose that?

General KEHLER. I would contrast—well, first of all, Senator, visibility and insight I think are tremendously important, as is the face-to-face contact that our inspectors and Russian inspectors get with counterparts and the way this forces us to interact.

I think over time, not just with New START but because of a number of agreements like this, we've developed a pretty comprehensive understanding of the Russians, and I think they've got a pretty comprehensive understanding of us, and that makes a difference perhaps in some places.

Senator HEINRICH. Which is important in a deterrence posture, right?

General KEHLER. Absolutely. It's important for deterrence, and I think it would be really important in a crisis.

Senator HEINRICH. If we pulled out or if Russia were to pull out of New START, would our strategic stability be improved, or would it be dramatically worse?

General KEHLER. Well, it depends.

Senator HEINRICH. Or somewhere in-between?

General KEHLER. I think it depends. I would contrast this interchange that we have with the Russians via arms control versus interchanges that we have with the Chinese, for example, over their forces, which we don't have really. One of the things that I always wanted to have was a military-to-military exchange with my counterparts in China, and we just were never able to make that happen.

There are things that I knew about the Russians and their nuclear forces and capabilities and safeguards and those kinds of things that I wished I had known about the Chinese. I think if you withdraw from those things, then——

Senator HEINRICH. Are they technical things, or technical things and a better understanding of intent and posture?

General KEHLER. Both. I've always believed that bringing us together in some way, military to military particularly but technical to technical as well, diplomacy to diplomacy, makes some sense. I don't believe, by the way, just to finish the thought, that this gets done at any cost. I think that there are consequences. If the Russians decide that they're going to cheat, then I think there ought to be consequences about that.

Senator HEINRICH. What do you see as the priorities for the next administrator at [National Security Administration] NSA in order to sustain the stockpile and assure that the NSA labs have the capabilities that they need to meet our military requirements?

General KEHLER. I think they've got to stay on the pathway. There have been issues, as I know the subcommittee is well aware of the issues that there have been to modernize the weapons complex. That is a unique, one-of-a-kind industrial complex. It does something that no other industrial complex can do. I think the investment in that is very important, but there have been real concerns about the costs of that modernization and how it's been carried out, *et cetera.*

I think that, like with any major acquisition, we've got to settle on some requirements, we've got to slap the table, and then we've got to invest in it and get going.

Senator HEINRICH. Interrelated with that, as you're well aware, Los Alamos Lab is the designated Center of Excellence for plutonium research. In your view, does our current plutonium strategy maintain the critical skills and the capability to support that modernization and production of plutonium?

General KEHLER. I think so. At least when I left the movie two-plus years ago, I thought we were on the right pathway. I am concerned about the skill set writ large. It's not just about plutonium. It's about keeping design skills in the complex. It's about keeping other skills in the complex. Just doing life extension programs doesn't necessarily keep it in the complex. If the complex is a hedge strategy for us, which is what we've said, then my view is it's not wise for us to be a nuclear power with no capability to produce a weapon if we ever had to.

Senator HEINRICH. For all three of you, earlier this week we saw North Korea launch four ballistic missiles that traveled approximately 1,000 kilometers towards Japan. The missiles landed about 200 miles from their coastline in the Sea of Japan. Do you believe that our missile defense system now deployed in South Korea serves as an effective deterrent? How could other capabilities, capabilities like cyber or directed energy, change the calculus of our adversaries in terms of missile defense? That's for whoever, jump ball. Not all at once.

Dr. SAMORE. I'll start. It's very difficult to defend South Korea, because even if you had in place an effective missile defense system, it's so vulnerable to artillery and rockets——

Senator HEINRICH. It's right there, 30 miles from the border.

Dr. SAMORE.—that any conflict would be devastating to our Korean allies. I do think that THAAD is justified because of the North Korean threat beyond Seoul, and also including United States military bases there. I can't answer the military question of whether the current battery is sufficient. The North Koreans, as you say, demonstrated earlier this week that they can fire a salvo of liquid-fueled systems. As they develop their solid-fueled systems, they will be even more capable.

Missile defense is not going to be the complete answer to defending Korea. I think there's a different situation with the United States. I think for the foreseeable future, North Korea's ability to attack the United States with long-range missiles is going to be very rudimentary. This is not Russia or China in terms of resources and technical capability.

I think our investment in national missile defense, including regional components, is a reasonable strategy for trying to defend ourselves if there should be war. I still think deterrence is an incredibly important feature of preventing war from breaking out, and I think the North Koreans recognize that they would be destroyed in a conflict. There's a strong incentive on their part not to start a war. It could escalate from a local conflict, and I think that's why it's so important that we invest in national missile defense against a limited threat from North Korea.

Senator HEINRICH. Thank you all.

Senator FISCHER. Thank you, Senator.

Senator Cotton?

Senator COTTON. Thank you.

I want to go back over some of the previous answers and questions and clarify or elaborate on some.

General Kehler, you mentioned slapping the table when it came to intermediate-range nuclear forces treaty violations by Russia. We've now done that. Our Government has said repeatedly that Russia is in violation of that treaty, although we haven't done much more than slap the table.

Could you explain to us the military significance of Russia possessing a ground-launched cruise missile system, one that is apparently road mobile as well, and maybe also how the United States and NATO should consider responding to such a blatant violation of the INF Treaty?

General KEHLER. Senator, I think the military impact of that at some level remains to be seen. It remains to be seen how many they deploy, how they go about doing this. Assuming for a moment that they deploy some number of these, I think it has implications for us in many ways. It has implications for the alliance in many ways, just like deployment of intermediate-range nuclear forces did during the Cold War. I think that the alliance will have to make some determination about how to go forward.

I think there are a lot of things that can be done. Certainly, you can pursue all the avenues in the INF Treaty to try to get all of this back on some kind of track, and I don't know honestly where that is. Again, all I read about this is what I see in the paper, so I don't know where that process stands.

Another thing that you can do, of course, as Dr. Samore said earlier, you can enhance our conventional presence and capabilities in Europe. We can make sure that our nuclear commitment to the alliance and the alliance's nuclear commitment and all the pieces that go with that remain firm.

Ultimately, we can decide whether or not to deploy additional capabilities there, whether those are additional defensive capabilities that are specifically intended to deal with the cruise missile threat, or ultimately whether these are additional offensive capabilities that we would have to deploy. I think all of those need to be considered as we go forward here while diplomacy continues to work its way forward.

Senator COTTON. Dr. Payne, do you have anything to add to that question?

Dr. PAYNE. Yes. I think the Russian violation of the INF Treaty with the cruise missile actually is important because it gives them a capability that's neither short-range nor strategic to back up their escalate-to-deescalate threats. If we're going to engage in nuclear threats explicitly, which they are doing and have done vis-à-vis NATO, having that kind of option that doesn't require a short-range system to support it and doesn't require them going to their strategic forces to support it I believe is an important rung in the escalation ladder that they appear to be filling with that capability and for that purpose.

I believe it's a validation for them of their escalate-to-deescalate threat, which is something we need to counter and deny.

Senator COTTON. Dr. Samore?

Dr. SAMORE. Let me add one thing. Russia's violation of the INF Treaty frees us from any obligation to abide by the treaty. If we decided for military reasons that we needed to deploy systems that are currently prohibited by the treaty, I think we're free to do so. That's a military judgment that NATO should make. I also think it's important to recognize that there would be some political cost to doing that, that especially in Germany and the Netherlands and other countries this would be controversial.

We need to weigh the military benefits of deploying systems if they're necessary against the potential political complications and figure out a strategy for overcoming those political complications.

Senator COTTON. Thank you.

Dr. Samore, in your testimony you said that low-yield nuclear weapons are much more important to Russia than to the United States. Would you specify for the record why that's the case?

Dr. SAMORE. Well, it's really a reverse of the situation during the Cold War. During the Cold War, we saw the Russians as having a conventional advantage, and therefore we needed tactical nuclear weapons in order to counterbalance that advantage. The Russians now see NATO as having an advantage in the conventional area, and they see tactical nuclear weapons as necessary to balance that advantage.

Senator COTTON. Dr. Samore, you said that, quote, "we ought to be open to" at least research and possibly development of new low-yield nuclear weapons.

Dr. Payne, in your written statement, you seem to be open to research and development of all kinds of new nuclear capabilities, if necessary, given the threat we face.

Dr. PAYNE. I think we ought to be open to looking at it, but I particularly think that the very low-yield option is something we ought to consider. I agree with Dr. Samore on that.

Senator COTTON. General Kehler, do you agree with the two doctors?

General KEHLER. Again, I think whether or not we need to deploy a new nuclear weapon remains to be seen. What I would not want is to be sometime forward deciding that we need to do that and not have the ability to do it. I would——

Senator COTTON. In terms of the nuclear infrastructure?

General KEHLER. Yes. I would want to keep whatever work in the pipeline that is appropriate to keep the skill set there. Someone mentioned prototyping, *et cetera*. There might be some good ways that we can keep the right skill set there.

Senator COTTON. Dr. Samore, you said that North Korea's ability to attack the continental United States with a nuclear weapon will remain rudimentary. They're obviously developing their missile program rapidly. The number of launches has increased significantly. They have nuclear devices, clearly. They tested them.

Do you say rudimentary because of the difficulty of developing an ICBM, or because of the difficulty of taking the third step of marrying those two technologies together, miniaturizing the warhead and having a suitable reentry vehicle?

Dr. SAMORE. That's correct, Senator. The North Koreans have not yet demonstrated the ability to have an effective reentry vehicle that could survive a long-range delivery. Until they do that, they don't really have a credible capability to attack us with a missile. Even if they do demonstrate that eventually, there are going to be limits on the numbers of ICBMs the North Koreans can deploy, on the kind of penetration aids they have, whether they have maneuverable warheads. All of this kind of high-technology end I think is nothing that the North Koreans can achieve in the near term, and therefore I think missile defense has a reasonable prospect of defeating their missile capability.

Senator COTTON. Of all the steps that you would take, from a standing stock to being able to hold at risk the continental United States with a nuclear-armed ICBM, is that last step of marrying the nuclear device and the missile in a suitable reentry vehicle the hardest technical step to take?

Dr. SAMORE. Well, it's the one they haven't been able to demonstrate yet. I'm not sure I would necessarily say it's the hardest, but the North Koreans have never tested a reentry vehicle at that range. It's something we don't know whether or not they're capable of, and probably they don't either.

Senator COTTON. Thank you, gentlemen.

Senator FISCHER. Senator Warren?

Senator WARREN. Thank you, Madam Chair.

Thank you all for being here.

I'd like to start by asking about the Iran nuclear deal. Our list of problems with Iran is long. Iran sponsors terrorism, they engage in human rights abuses, test missiles, and take a lot of destabilizing actions in their part of the world. Given what Iran is willing to do, I think it's a lot easier to counter their provocative actions so long as Iran does not have nuclear weapons than it would be to try to cabin Iran if they possessed a nuclear weapon.

Now, we forced Iran to the negotiating table with international sanctions, and so far this nuclear deal has blocked Iran's path to the bomb while putting in place an unprecedented inspections regime. Now President Trump says he wants to ignore all of this and instead he has threatened to rip up the Iran nuclear deal. It's not just our deal with Iran. The agreement includes Britain, France, Germany, Russia, China, and the European Union. He can't rip it up. What he can do is abandon the deal unilaterally.

So, Dr. Samore, if the United States unilaterally withdraws from the deal, how easy would it be to convince our allies to re-impose sanctions on Iran?

Dr. SAMORE. Well, I think it would be very difficult because they would hold us responsible for blowing up an agreement which they believe is working to constrain Iran's nuclear program, despite all the other objections we have to Iranian behavior. My concern, if we unilaterally abrogated the agreement, is that we would find ourselves in a very weak position to restore the kind of sanctions that forced Iran to negotiate in the first place.

Senator WARREN. That's right. Without those sanctions, what are the chances we're going to get Iran to negotiate a better deal from our perspective?

Dr. SAMORE. Well, the trouble with not having leverage in a negotiation is that we might quickly be forced to have to use military options. You'd have to be prepared to use military force in that event.

Senator WARREN. If the deal collapsed, do you believe that the Iranians would likely resume their nuclear program?

Dr. SAMORE. I think so, but I think they'd be very cautious. I mean, if you look at the history of Iran's program, they could be much more technically advanced than they are now in terms of producing weapons-grade uranium and so forth. I think the Iranians have tried to calculate how can we move the program forward without inviting a military attack or strong international reaction. I think they would probably revive the program. The restraints would be lifted. I don't think they'd race for a bomb. I think they're much too cautious for that.

Senator WARREN. It sounds like to me that enforcing the deal we have is better than not having a deal.

Dr. SAMORE. I think so, and I think as the Trump Administration reviews their options my guess is that they will probably conclude that it makes sense to continue to abide by the deal as long as Iran does.

Senator WARREN. I hope so.

Let me ask you another part about this. The International Atomic Energy Agency is responsible for monitoring and inspections of Iran's nuclear program. The United States is the largest contributor to this nuclear watchdog budget, and many of our allies also contribute.

According to media reports and a leaked draft executive order, President Trump is considering a significant cut to U.S. funding for international organizations like the [International Atomic Energy Agency] IAEA by as much as 40 percent, and this is despite the fact that a GAO report issued last June explained that IAEA officials will need about $10 million more each year, in addition to the funding they have over the next 15 years, to fund the verification and monitoring of Iran's nuclear program.

So, Dr. Samore, regardless of what anyone's opinion is about the Iran deal, does cutting the IAEA's resources for verifying Iran's compliance with the agreement increase or decrease the likelihood of Iran developing a nuclear bomb?

Dr. SAMORE. Well, if we cut the IAEA's resources, they will be less able to monitor Iran's program, and therefore the Iranians might calculate they have a greater likelihood of not being caught if they cheated. I might add the IAEA, of course, does more than monitor Iran's program. They monitor peaceful nuclear programs all around the world.

Senator WARREN. The impact is everywhere.

Dr. SAMORE. The impact would be everywhere, yes.

Senator WARREN. Thank you.

The nuclear deal put in place put an unprecedented inspections regime on Iran, and that regime has provided tools that we didn't have before to help prevent a nuclear-armed Iran. If that's actually our goal, it seems to me that it would make sense that we would want the nuclear agency that's charged with monitoring this to have the tools that it needs to be able to do its job.

I made a note here that Secretary of Defense Mattis was and is a critic of the Iran nuclear deal. During his confirmation he made the point to our committee, when America gives her word, we have to live up to it and work with our allies, and I think that's particularly true when our allies are signaling that they're going to ignore us if we throw a fit and start to walk away from the deal. If we're serious about reducing the threat of nuclear proliferation, then I think the United States should make sure that the entire world understands that it is Iran's fault if this deal falls apart.

I want to take the last minute I've got, if I can, just to follow up on a question about North Korea. We've talked about the threat from North Korea. By my count, they've conducted five nuclear tests since 2006. We talked about that last week. They test-launched four missiles in the Sea of Japan. These are real threats from a dangerous, unstable, and nuclear-armed state.

Refusing to talk to North Korea over the last several years has not stopped their extreme behavior, and despite the tough sanctions they continue these provocative actions.

The question I want to ask about is that North Korea relies heavily on its ally, China, and in recent months the Chinese Government has signaled some frustration with the North Korean Government and suspended all North Korean coal imports, which is a major source of income for the regime.

Dr. Samore, do you think the Chinese strategy towards North Korea has changed? Is that what we're seeing here?

I'll be careful about my time here, Madam Chair.

Dr. SAMORE. I think the Chinese are terribly frustrated and angry with Kim Jong Un, and they're signaling to him that if he continues to carry out testing that damages China's interests they will punish him by exacting economic penalties. From that standpoint I think the Chinese are working with us better than they ever had before. At the end of the day I think the Chinese will not be willing to pull the economic plug on North Korea. I think China is too worried about instability.

We're going to have to figure out whether we want to use the economic leverage that we've acquired in order to try to negotiate some limits on North Korea's nuclear missile program. I'm not terribly optimistic that will work. We've tried three times in the past and the North Koreans have always violated or cheated or reneged on the agreement, but I do think it's worth another try to slow down their effort to develop an ICBM.

Senator WARREN. I take it from this, it is important to bring as much pressure as we can bear on China to try to get China to bring more pressure on North Korea to try to get them to abide by some kind of control agreement.

Dr. SAMORE. Well, and to develop a common strategy with China, because even though the United States and China have different fundamental strategic interests on the Korean Peninsula, both of us have a common interest in preventing or limiting North Korea's nuclear and missile program.

Senator WARREN. Thank you very much, I appreciate it.

Thank you, Madam Chair, for your indulgence.

Senator FISCHER. Senator Peters?

Senator PETERS. Thank you, Madam Chair.

Thank you to our witnesses here today.

I have a question related to ballistic missile defense, particularly continental defense and the location of continental interceptor sites. Being the senator from Michigan, we are under consideration for one of those sites, along with Ohio, New York, in addition to what we have in California and in Alaska. I just want to get a sense from one or all of you as to the importance of locating a site at one of those three places to complement what we currently have existing. Is it something that we need to be moving forward with, particularly perhaps in light of what we're seeing in Korea, but in addition to the sophisticated missile system that the Chinese have, and others?

Dr. PAYNE. I'll go ahead. I think it is important, sir. The recent discussion we just had about North Korea emphasizes both, I believe, the need to have what I described earlier in my testimony as a capability to prevent limited nuclear strike options, particularly vis-à-vis North Korea, but vis-à-vis others as well.

Moving in that direction in my mind is very important because I don't believe that North Korea is going to allow its nuclear capability to be rolled back. I don't think China is actually ever going to press hard enough to do that. It's going to continue to expand its nuclear capabilities. It's going to continue to expand its missile capabilities.

We see this going in one direction, and that site east of the Mississippi is going to be important for expanding our ability to protect the United States.

Senator PETERS. Do others of you agree? It can be a short answer. General, do you agree?

General KEHLER. I would agree, with a caveat. I think we always have the option to deploy additional missile defenses. I would be very interested in how additional steps that we take now would be oriented toward dealing with the threat from North Korea. I think that's the priority.

Senator PETERS. Okay, thank you.

Dr. SAMORE. I don't feel qualified to answer.

Senator PETERS. Okay, that's fine.

Back to the Russian situation and the deployment of this intermediate-range missile in violation of the treaty, which I think is very disturbing. I find it curious and I'd just like to have your reaction, that when we talk about the New [Strategic Arms Reduction] START Treaty, the Russian compliance has been pretty good over the years, and there have been news reports that Mr. Putin has raised the possibility of extending it with President Trump, so those discussions are going on now.

At the same time that that's going on, they are pretty blatantly violating another treaty at the same time. In your view, why do the Russians choose to violate one while remaining in compliance with the other? What's the strategic calculus there?

Dr. SAMORE. Well, the Russians have complained about the INF Treaty for many years because their argument was it only constrains the United States and Russia and doesn't constrain other countries that have missiles in that intermediate range, and for years now the Russians have proposed that we try to globalize the INF Treaty, which I think is not a practical suggestion because those other countries wouldn't agree. The Russians have felt compelled for their military reasons to want to deploy systems that are prohibited by the INF Treaty.

Now, they're perfectly allowed under the treaty to withdraw from the treaty if they feel it's no longer in their interests and openly deploy those systems. In typical Russian fashion, instead of doing the above-board thing, which is to withdraw from the treaty, just like we withdrew from the [Anti-Ballistic Missile] ABM Treaty, the Russians do it by cheating and denial, and that's the practice we've seen. The reason they comply with New START is because they see it in their interest. The reason why they violate INF is because they see it in their interest.

Dr. PAYNE. I agree with that. The only other point that I would make is that the Russians are not just in violation of the INF Treaty. They're in violation of a whole series of treaties, and I frankly am not entirely confident that the Russians are going to meet their obligations to meet the New START ceilings next February. I hope that's the case, but they are so far above the warhead ceiling now that they're going to have to do some serious withdrawal of capabilities to meet that ceiling. We'll see whether it happens or not.

General KEHLER. I just agree with my colleagues.

Senator PETERS. What you're saying is that we can't trust the Russians. It's pretty clear. They're not our friend on many, many occasions, and we have to be concerned about it.

I'll switch gears to overall proliferation. Dr. Samore, you mentioned the weapon states that are out there, the nine that have weapons now, and there's a list—I believe it's close to 30 countries that have peaceful nuclear programs, somewhere in that range. I'm concerned about the Iranian deal in the fact of what's going to happen in 10 to 15 years when they can get back to scaling up the enrichment of uranium, which is certainly one of the paths to weaponization.

The United States has had a fairly consistent policy, I think, in the past, that although we support the use of peaceful power and believe that every nation has a right to peaceful nuclear power, we have not said a nation has the right to enrich uranium.

To what extent are you concerned that some of the other countries who may have peaceful programs now and don't enrich will start enriching? That could lead to an increased proliferation risk. I believe the Canadians have that option and they actually decided against it, not because we were concerned or that anyone had any concern that the Canadians were going to weaponize themselves, but they thought just the fact that they were enriching uranium provided a proliferation risk that was unacceptable.

I'm concerned about the other nations out there, and I'm hearing Brazil and other countries may be interested in doing that. Where does that path lead, and do we need to take some steps to constrain the ability to enrich uranium, which would be helpful for us to prevent the Iranians from doing it as well in 10 to 15 years?

To any of the panelists, how should we be thinking about dealing with this slowly creeping proliferation risk that I think is out there?

Dr. SAMORE. You know, it's a very good question, Senator. We've always been inconsistent in our policy about enrichment. We have accepted that certain close allies will develop enrichment for peaceful purposes, Japan and Europe for example, and we've always tried to draw the line, no new countries developing enrichment, which is very difficult. In the case of Brazil, for example, the Bush Administration decided not to object to Brazil pursuing a peaceful enrichment program.

I think you're right to be worried about the precedent that the Iran deal will set, although as I read the deal and as I've talked to the negotiators, in 15 years if Iran seeks to build an industrial-scale enrichment plant and we think they still harbor ambitions to develop nuclear weapons, we have the option to object to that. We're not required to acquiesce. I think the nuclear deal in 15 years, if it lasts that long, will have to face that issue, will have to face that problem.

Senator PETERS. Thank you so much, appreciate it.

Senator FISCHER. Thank you, Senator Peters.

My thanks to the panel today for the information you've provided to us, and we certainly appreciate your thoughtful comments as well.

With that, the hearing is adjourned.

[Whereupon, at 4:03 p.m., the hearing was adjourned.]

○

www.ingramcontent.com/pod-product-compliance
Lightning Source LLC
Chambersburg PA
CBHW080048260726
48658CB00007B/2800